D1068312

PICTURE BOOK OF

LOUISIANA

By

BERNADINE BAILEY

Pictures by

KURT WIESE

ALBERT WHITMAN AND COMPANY

CHICAGO ILLINOIS

Published simultaneously
in the Dominion of Canada
by George J. McLeod, Ltd., Toronto

Lithographed in the U.S.A.
Library of Congress Catalog
Card No. 54-9944

LOUISIANA
Caddo Lake
SHREVEPORT
MONROE
Red River
MISSISSIPPI RIVER
NATCHITOCHES
PINEVILLE
ALEXANDRIA
OPELOUSAS
LAKE CHARLES
LAFAYETTE
BATON ROUGE
Lake Pontchartrain
NEW ORLEANS
GULF OF MEXICO

Shaped like a huge boot with its toe dipping into the Gulf, the state of Louisiana has a charm all its own. On the east lies Mississippi, on the west is Texas, to the north is Arkansas, and to the south is the Gulf of Mexico.

Of the total area of 48,522 square miles, 3,361 square miles are water: rivers, bayous, lakes, lagoons, and flooded marshlands. Lake Pontchartrain is the largest body of water within the state.

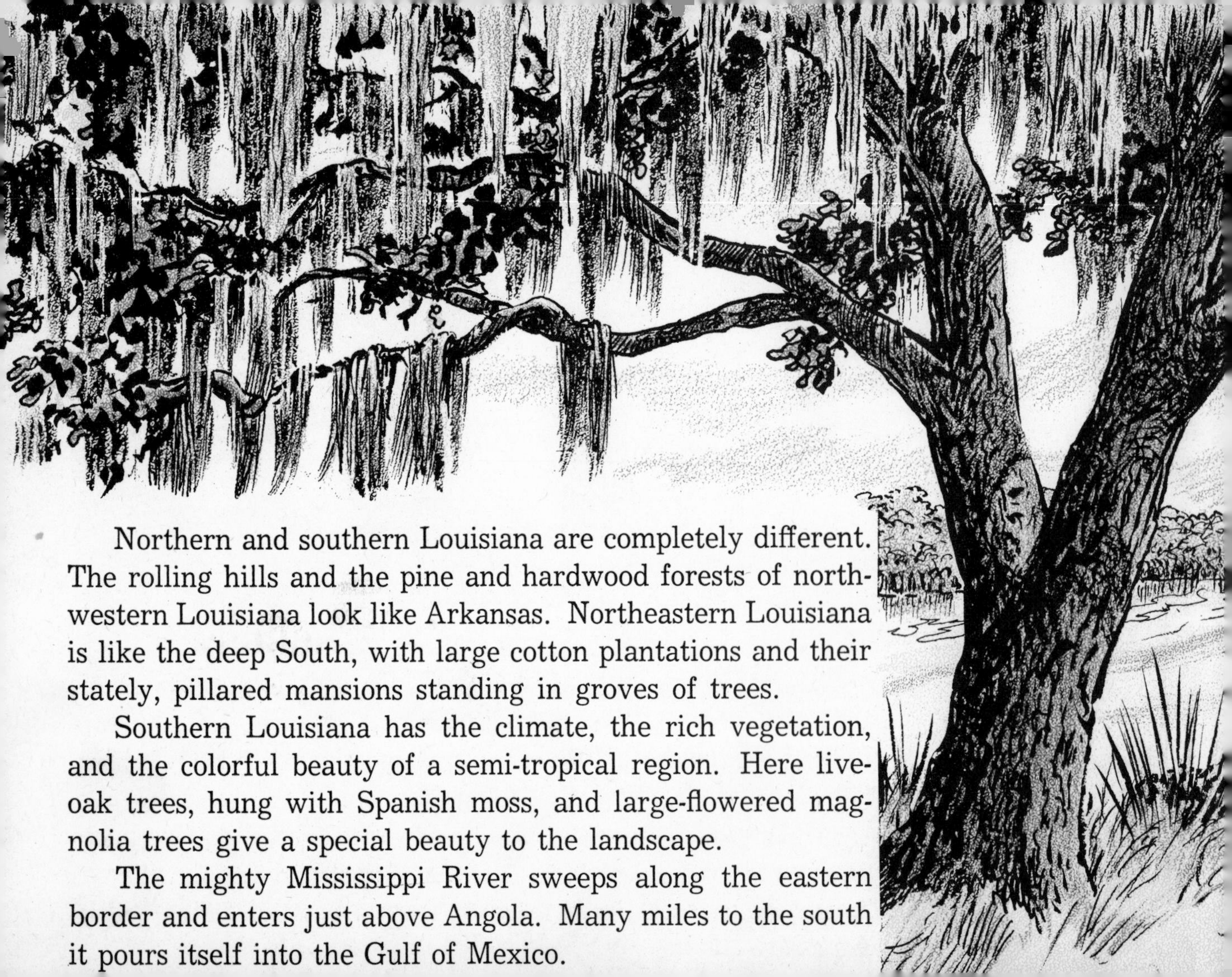

Northern and southern Louisiana are completely different. The rolling hills and the pine and hardwood forests of northwestern Louisiana look like Arkansas. Northeastern Louisiana is like the deep South, with large cotton plantations and their stately, pillared mansions standing in groves of trees.

Southern Louisiana has the climate, the rich vegetation, and the colorful beauty of a semi-tropical region. Here live-oak trees, hung with Spanish moss, and large-flowered magnolia trees give a special beauty to the landscape.

The mighty Mississippi River sweeps along the eastern border and enters just above Angola. Many miles to the south it pours itself into the Gulf of Mexico.

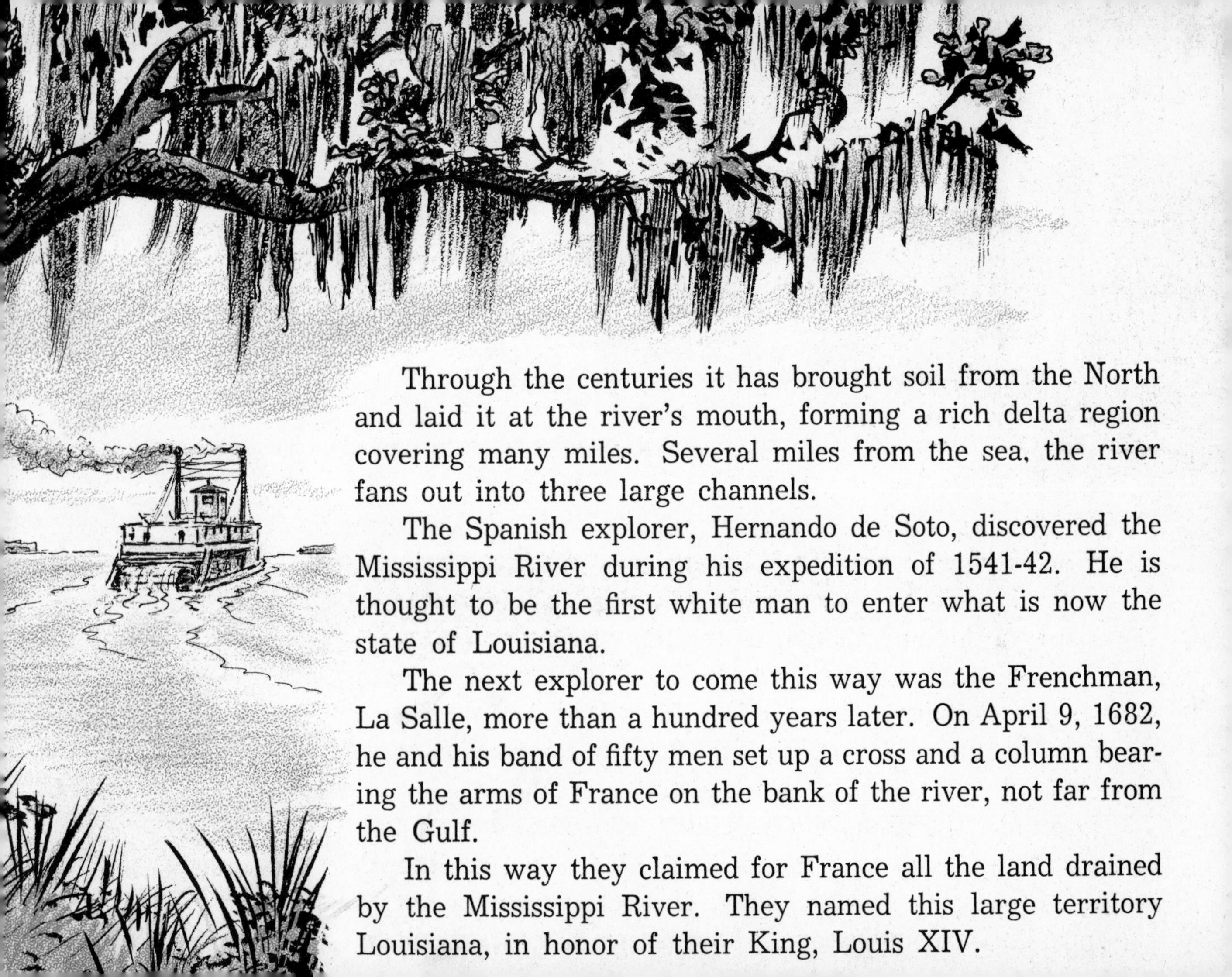

Through the centuries it has brought soil from the North and laid it at the river's mouth, forming a rich delta region covering many miles. Several miles from the sea, the river fans out into three large channels.

The Spanish explorer, Hernando de Soto, discovered the Mississippi River during his expedition of 1541-42. He is thought to be the first white man to enter what is now the state of Louisiana.

The next explorer to come this way was the Frenchman, La Salle, more than a hundred years later. On April 9, 1682, he and his band of fifty men set up a cross and a column bearing the arms of France on the bank of the river, not far from the Gulf.

In this way they claimed for France all the land drained by the Mississippi River. They named this large territory Louisiana, in honor of their King, Louis XIV.

Fur traders and missionaries continued the work of exploration, always trying to make friends with the Indians. In 1712, the French government gave all trading rights in Louisiana to Antoine Crozat, a wealthy merchant.

In 1717, Crozat transferred these rights to John Law, head of the Company of the Indies. This trader painted such a glowing picture of Louisiana, that hundreds of settlers came here from Europe, hoping to make their fortune.

To protect the Louisiana Territory from attacks by Spain and England, a city was founded, in 1718, near the mouth of the Mississippi. It was named New Orleans in honor of Philippe, the Duke of Orleans, who was then Regent of France.

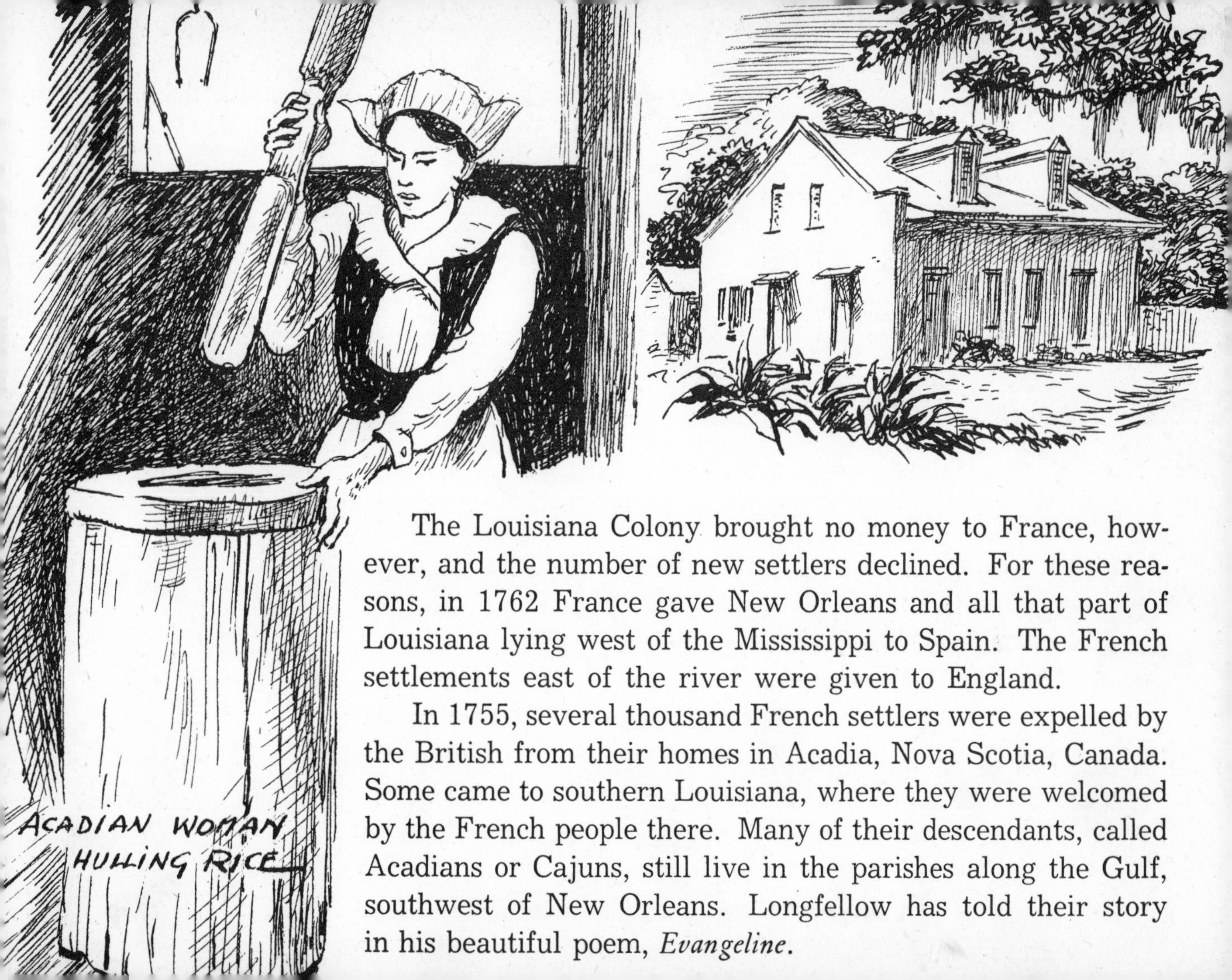

The Louisiana Colony brought no money to France, however, and the number of new settlers declined. For these reasons, in 1762 France gave New Orleans and all that part of Louisiana lying west of the Mississippi to Spain. The French settlements east of the river were given to England.

In 1755, several thousand French settlers were expelled by the British from their homes in Acadia, Nova Scotia, Canada. Some came to southern Louisiana, where they were welcomed by the French people there. Many of their descendants, called Acadians or Cajuns, still live in the parishes along the Gulf, southwest of New Orleans. Longfellow has told their story in his beautiful poem, *Evangeline*.

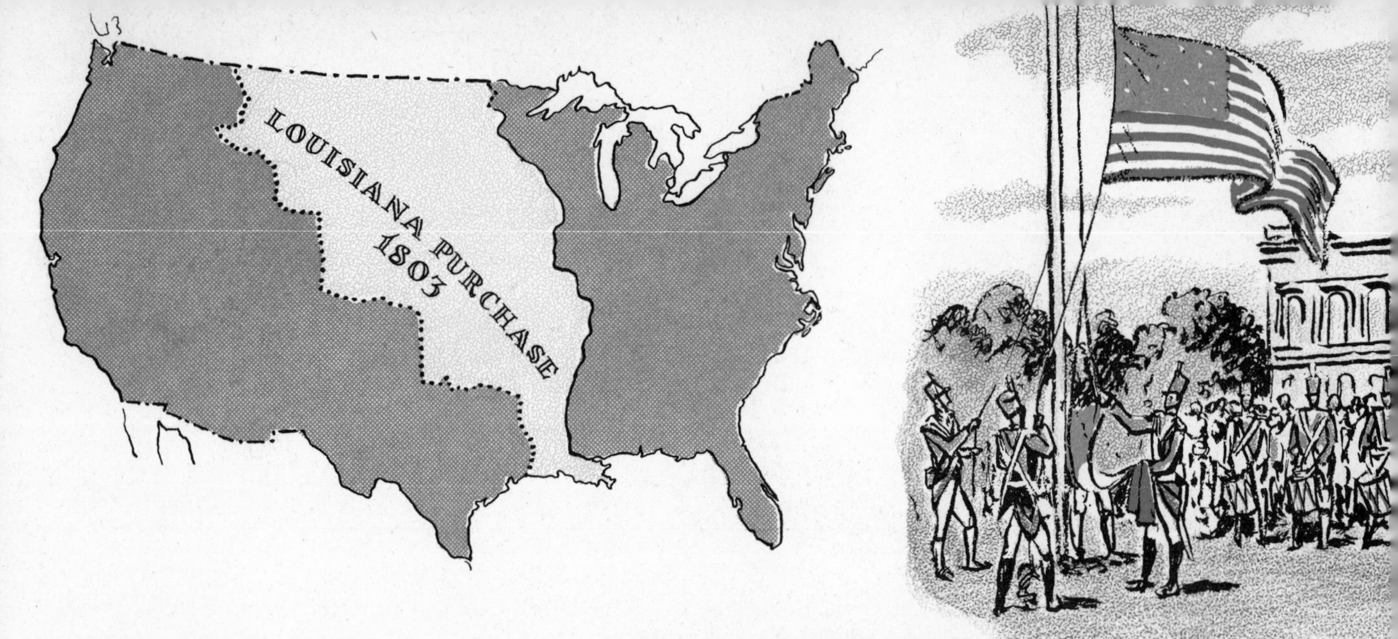

When the American colonies revolted against England, Spain took the side of the colonies. In 1779, war broke out between Spain and England. Bernardo de Galvez, Spanish governor of Louisiana, captured Baton Rouge and other cities belonging to England. Thus in 1781, all the area that is now the state of Louisiana came under one flag, the Spanish.

Spanish rule lasted only twenty years, however. In 1801, by the Treaty of San Idlefonso, Spain gave Louisiana back to France. This nation owned it for two years. On April 30, 1803, Napoleon, Emperor of France, sold the Louisiana Territory to the United States for $15 million dollars.

The white descendants of the early French and Spanish settlers were called Creoles. They were not happy about the invasion of the crude traders and river men from the North. Their customs and culture, their language and education were very different from those of the pioneer Americans.

In April, 1812, the Creole State became the eighteenth state to join the Union, with New Orleans as its first capital.

The Battle of New Orleans

The famous Battle of New Orleans took place on January 8, 1815. At this time, General Andrew Jackson led a force of American recruits from Louisiana, Kentucky, Tennessee, and Mississippi against a British force commanded by General Sir Edward Pakenham.

Aided by the Lafittes and other pirates, Jackson's troops completely routed the British. The War of 1812, between England and the United States, had already ended on December 24, 1814, but the news did not reach General Jackson for many days.

With the invention of the steamboat, New Orleans became an important port. Ships poured into the city, bringing both passengers and freight. Towns sprang up along the banks of the Mississippi, where cotton from the plantations was loaded on board for shipping.

When Captain Henry Shreve cleared the Red River of its mass of driftwood, it became an important avenue of commerce and attracted many settlers to northwestern Louisiana. In 1837, the Captain and seven others founded the city of Shreveport.

Louisiana seceded from the Union on January 26, 1861, and remained an independent republic, under its own flag, for six weeks. Then it joined the other states of the Confederacy in the War between the States.

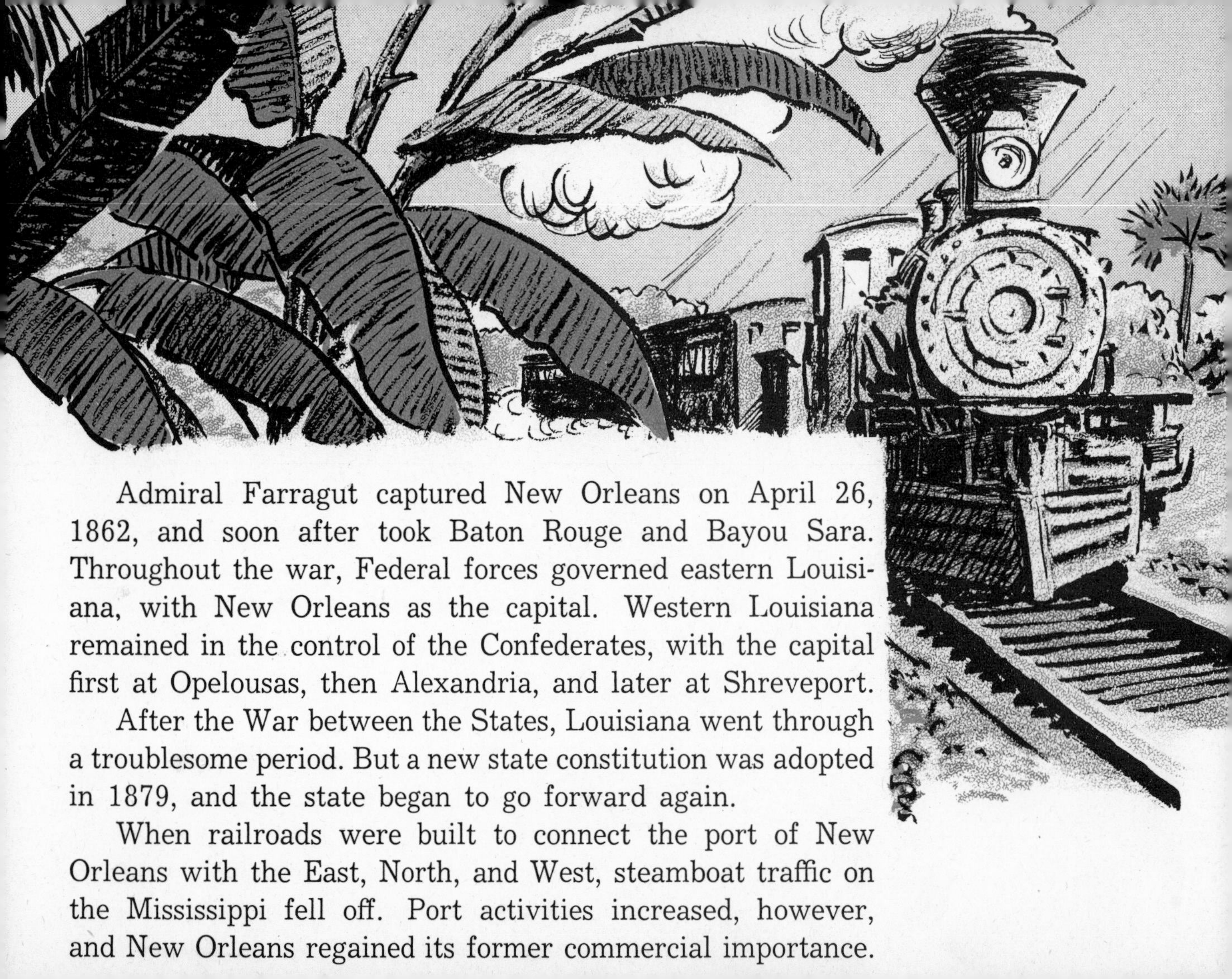

Admiral Farragut captured New Orleans on April 26, 1862, and soon after took Baton Rouge and Bayou Sara. Throughout the war, Federal forces governed eastern Louisiana, with New Orleans as the capital. Western Louisiana remained in the control of the Confederates, with the capital first at Opelousas, then Alexandria, and later at Shreveport.

After the War between the States, Louisiana went through a troublesome period. But a new state constitution was adopted in 1879, and the state began to go forward again.

When railroads were built to connect the port of New Orleans with the East, North, and West, steamboat traffic on the Mississippi fell off. Port activities increased, however, and New Orleans regained its former commercial importance.

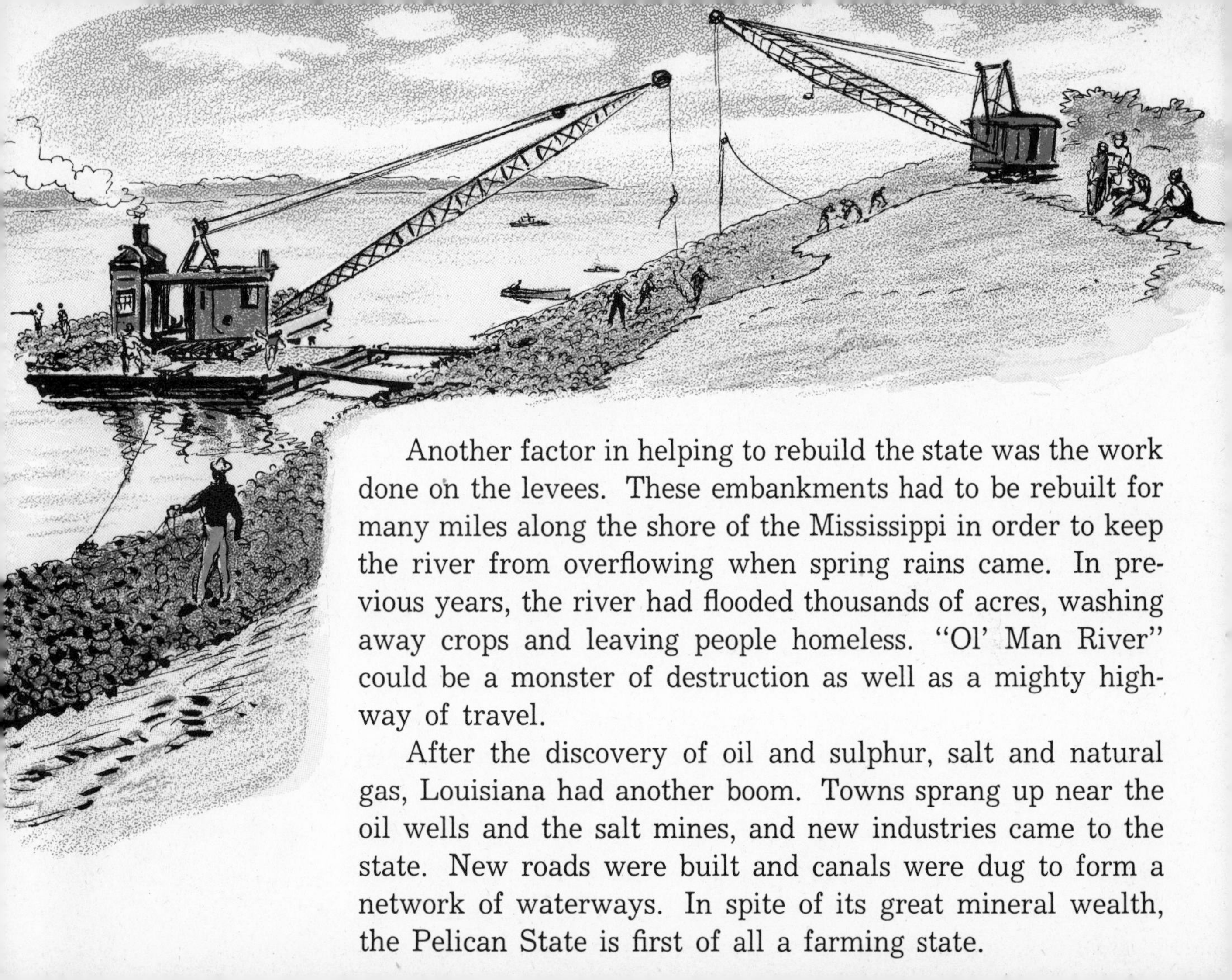

Another factor in helping to rebuild the state was the work done on the levees. These embankments had to be rebuilt for many miles along the shore of the Mississippi in order to keep the river from overflowing when spring rains came. In previous years, the river had flooded thousands of acres, washing away crops and leaving people homeless. "Ol' Man River" could be a monster of destruction as well as a mighty highway of travel.

After the discovery of oil and sulphur, salt and natural gas, Louisiana had another boom. Towns sprang up near the oil wells and the salt mines, and new industries came to the state. New roads were built and canals were dug to form a network of waterways. In spite of its great mineral wealth, the Pelican State is first of all a farming state.

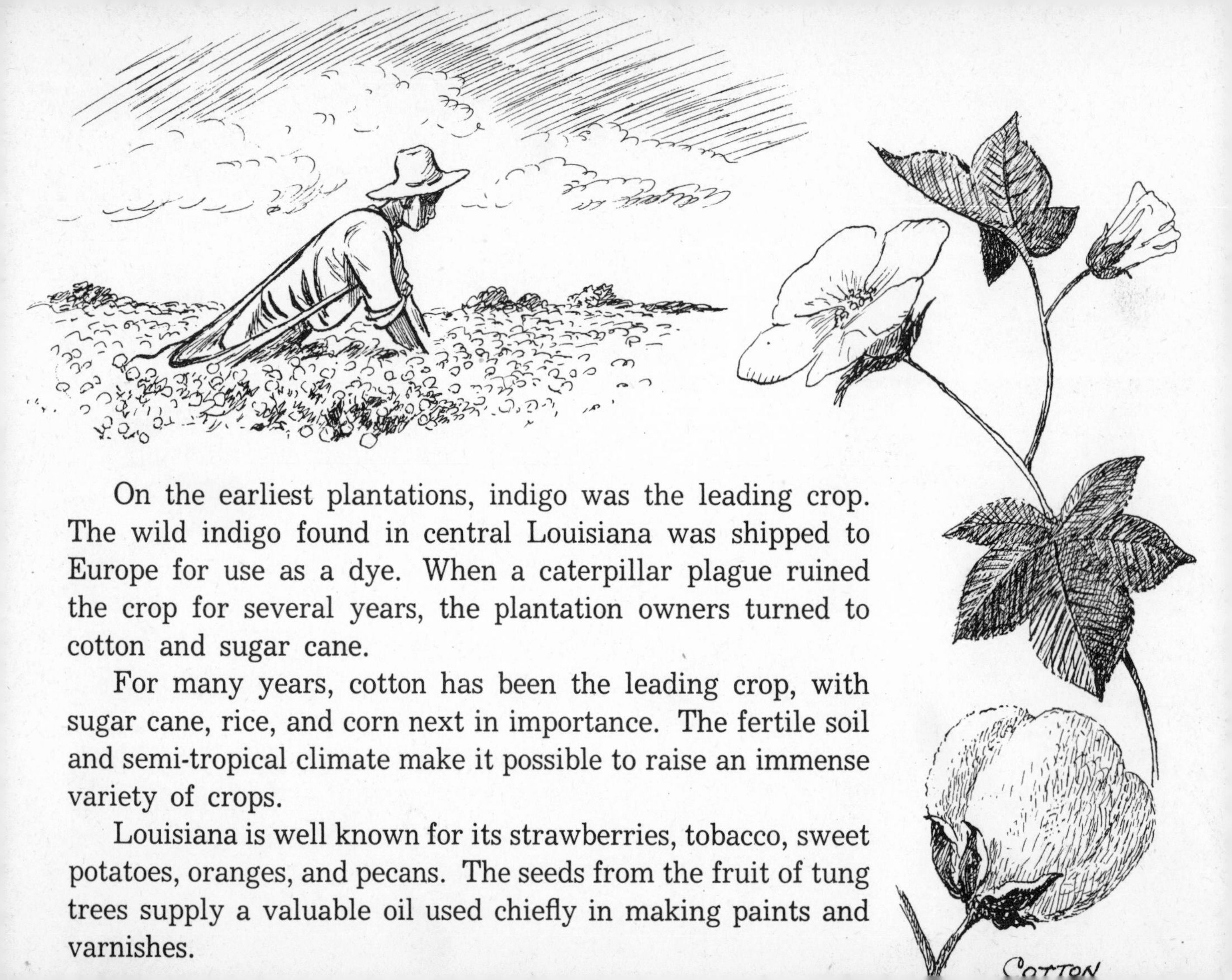

On the earliest plantations, indigo was the leading crop. The wild indigo found in central Louisiana was shipped to Europe for use as a dye. When a caterpillar plague ruined the crop for several years, the plantation owners turned to cotton and sugar cane.

For many years, cotton has been the leading crop, with sugar cane, rice, and corn next in importance. The fertile soil and semi-tropical climate make it possible to raise an immense variety of crops.

Louisiana is well known for its strawberries, tobacco, sweet potatoes, oranges, and pecans. The seeds from the fruit of tung trees supply a valuable oil used chiefly in making paints and varnishes.

Thousands of beef cattle graze on cut-over pinelands and on the marshy lands along the coast. Hogs are raised on farms throughout the state, but especially in the delta region. Sheep range on piney pasture land and produce thousands of pounds of wool each year.

Lakes yield an abundance of fresh fish. From the waters of the Gulf of Mexico come oysters and crabs. Shrimp also are caught in the Gulf. They are frozen or canned for shipment to markets throughout the country. The annual catch of shrimp alone is valued at many millions of dollars.

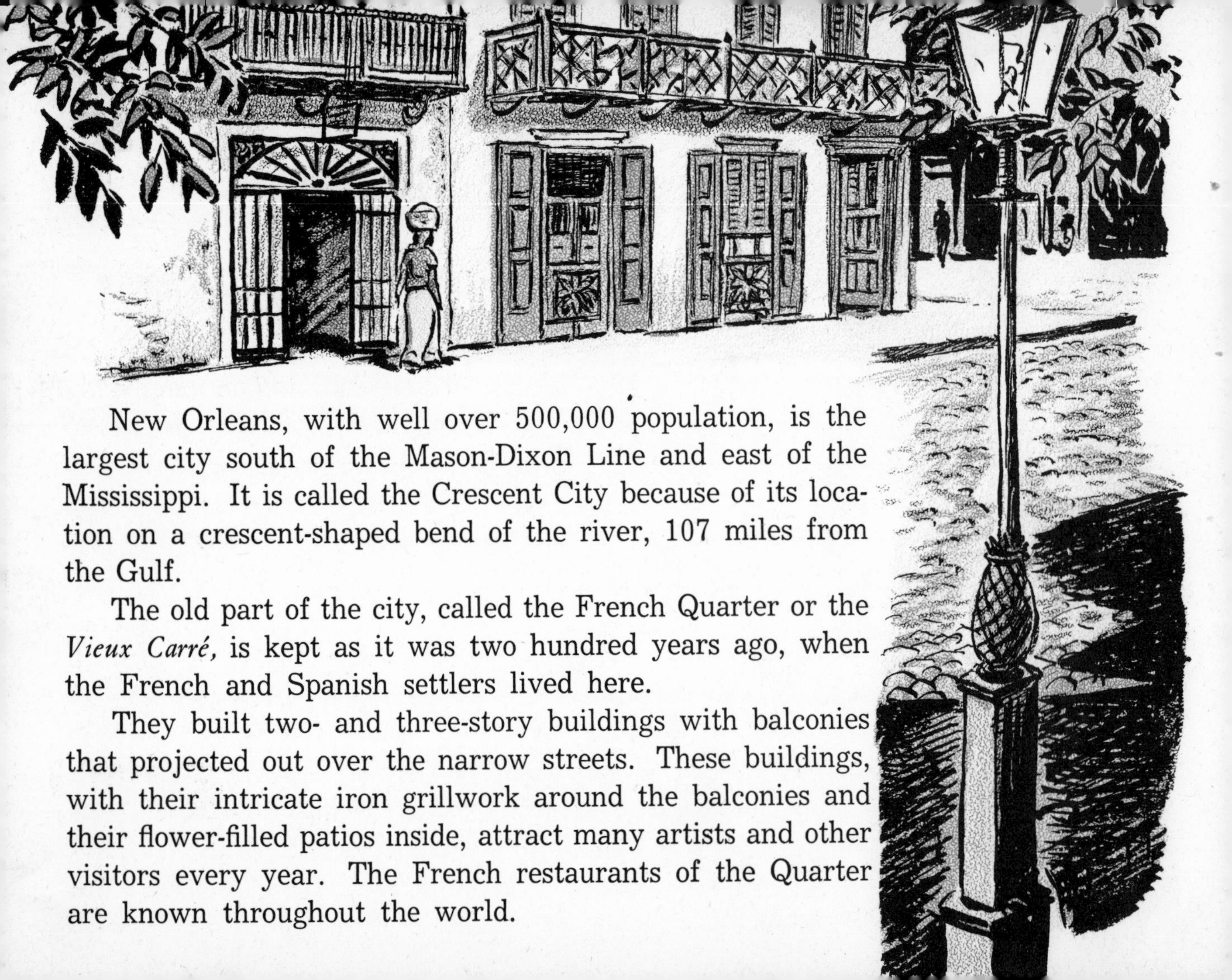

New Orleans, with well over 500,000 population, is the largest city south of the Mason-Dixon Line and east of the Mississippi. It is called the Crescent City because of its location on a crescent-shaped bend of the river, 107 miles from the Gulf.

The old part of the city, called the French Quarter or the *Vieux Carré,* is kept as it was two hundred years ago, when the French and Spanish settlers lived here.

They built two- and three-story buildings with balconies that projected out over the narrow streets. These buildings, with their intricate iron grillwork around the balconies and their flower-filled patios inside, attract many artists and other visitors every year. The French restaurants of the Quarter are known throughout the world.

In the heart of the French Quarter is Jackson Square, where many events took place that shaped the history of the city and the state. Of special interest here are the St. Louis Cathedral, and its neighbor building, the Cabildo, which was the seat of government when the Spanish controlled Louisiana.

Long famous for its gayety, New Orleans' fun reaches its climax every spring at the Mardi Gras festival. After several weeks of formal balls and other parties, there is an elaborate celebration on Shrove Tuesday (Mardi Gras). Magnificent floats and masked revelers in gay costumes parade down Canal Street, which is lighted by hundreds of oil flares. At midnight, the beginning of Lent, the merrymaking stops and the city goes back to normal.

Outside the French Quarter, New Orleans is an extremely modern city. Tulane University, Newcomb College and Ursuline College for Women, and Loyola University draw students from all over the South. Xavier University is a Catholic college entirely for Negroes.

Fifteen hundred acres comprise the area of City Park. Its playgrounds are a favorite place for picnickers, boaters, and fishermen. There are twenty-five baseball diamonds and two golf courses, besides a stadium seating many thousands.

Audubon Park, with its large zoo, is another popular recreation spot. So too is Lake Pontchartrain, just north of the city, where swimming is enjoyed throughout the long summer.

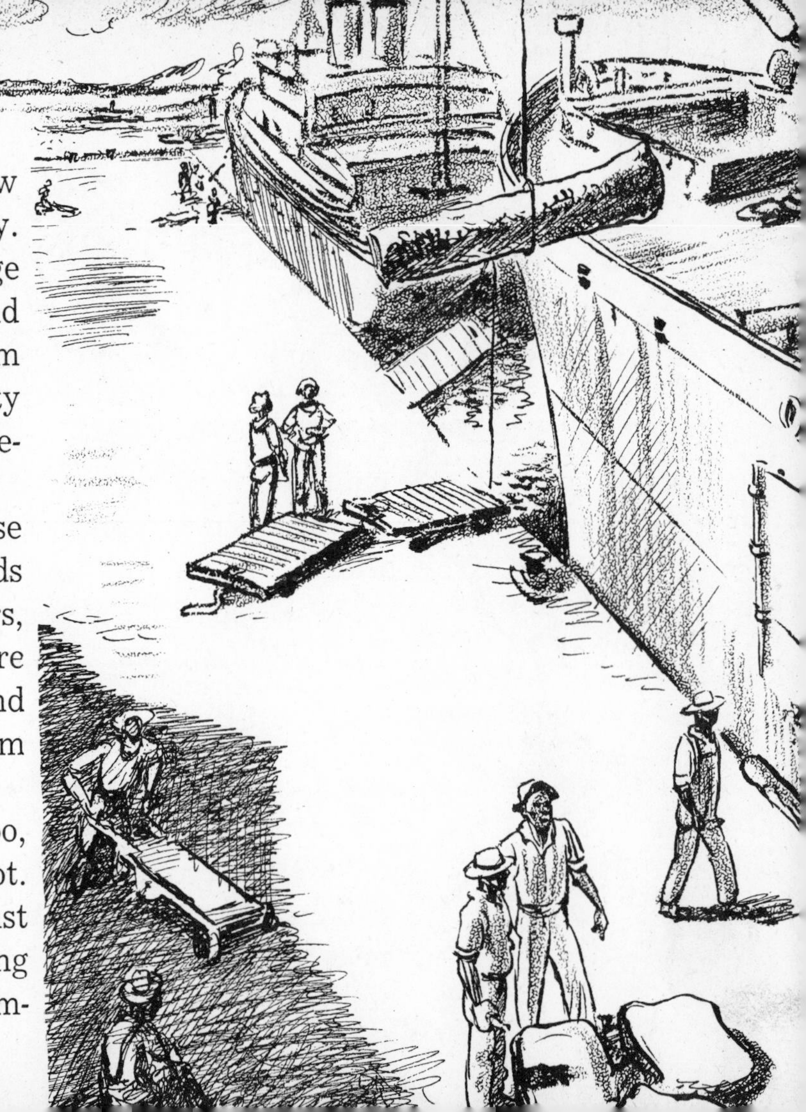

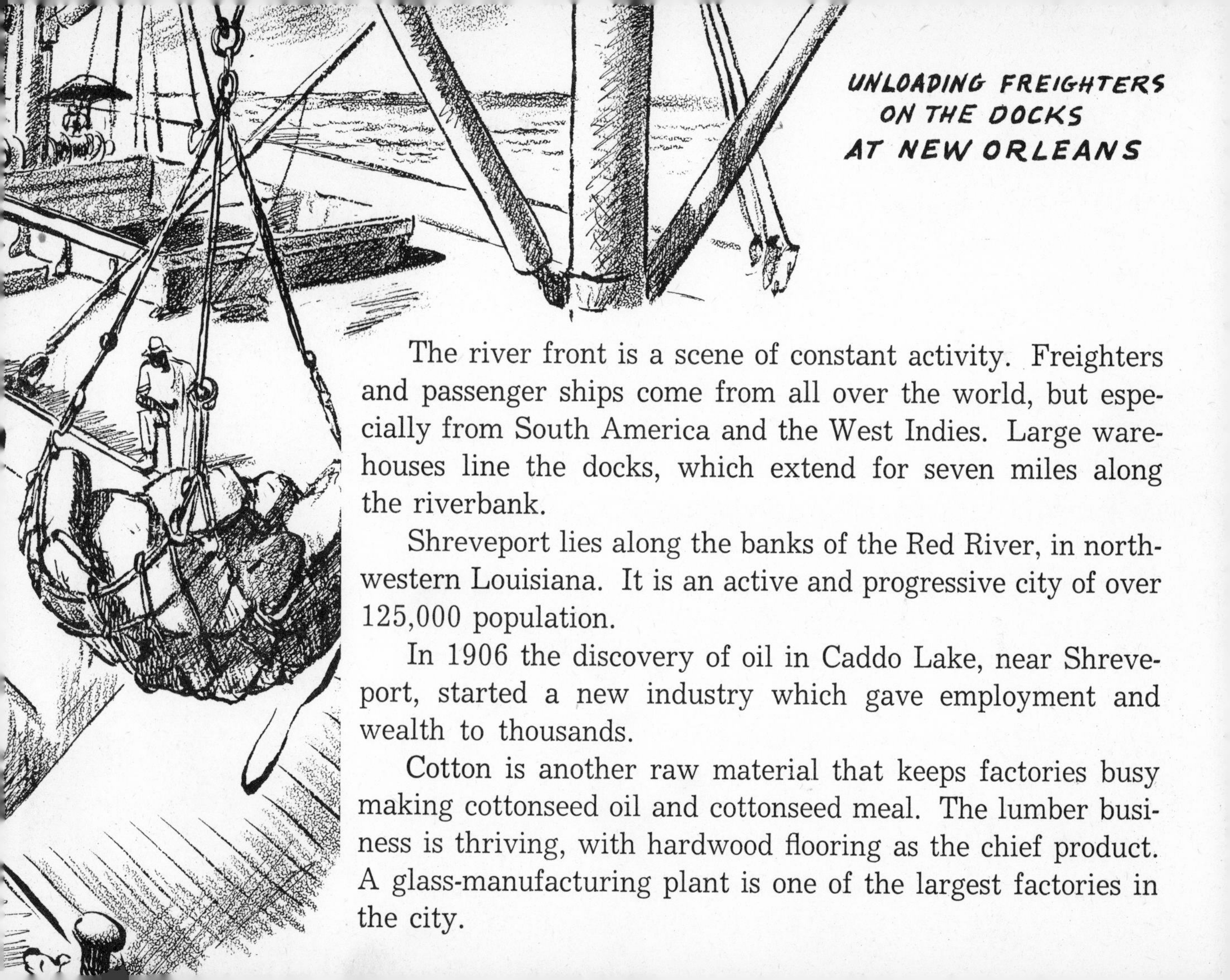

The river front is a scene of constant activity. Freighters and passenger ships come from all over the world, but especially from South America and the West Indies. Large warehouses line the docks, which extend for seven miles along the riverbank.

Shreveport lies along the banks of the Red River, in northwestern Louisiana. It is an active and progressive city of over 125,000 population.

In 1906 the discovery of oil in Caddo Lake, near Shreveport, started a new industry which gave employment and wealth to thousands.

Cotton is another raw material that keeps factories busy making cottonseed oil and cottonseed meal. The lumber business is thriving, with hardwood flooring as the chief product. A glass-manufacturing plant is one of the largest factories in the city.

THE STATE FLAG

Centenary College of Louisiana, St. Vincent's College, and Dodd College are all located in Shreveport.

Baton Rouge, the capital, has approximately the same population as Shreveport. It is built along a fifty-foot bluff on the east bank of the Mississippi, about seventy miles up the river from New Orleans.

With its many shady oaks, elms, and magnolias, the city seems to be set in a forest. Southern plantation homes and others of Spanish architecture give the city great beauty.

Baton Rouge was made the capital of Louisiana in 1849, but in 1862 it was captured by the Union troops and the capital was moved elsewhere.

The seat of government was returned to Baton Rouge in 1882. A new capitol, erected during the time of Governor Huey P. Long, is a striking building of marble and limestone, whose central tower rises 450 feet into the air.

Louisiana State University, in Baton Rouge, is one of the high-ranking universities of the South. Its campus of nearly five thousand acres has a two-mile frontage along the Mississippi, with many beautiful buildings built by Governor Long.

Men and women students come from many parts of the nation to study engineering and commerce, agriculture and law, the arts and sciences. Its School of Music is nationally known for its Opera Department.

Although it is far north from the Gulf of Mexico, Baton Rouge is a deep-water port with a 35-foot river channel. Chemicals, crude oil, and petroleum products, as well as sugar cane, cotton, and strawberries are shipped to many American and foreign ports. River barges carry goods to and from Chicago, Minneapolis, Pittsburgh, and points in between.

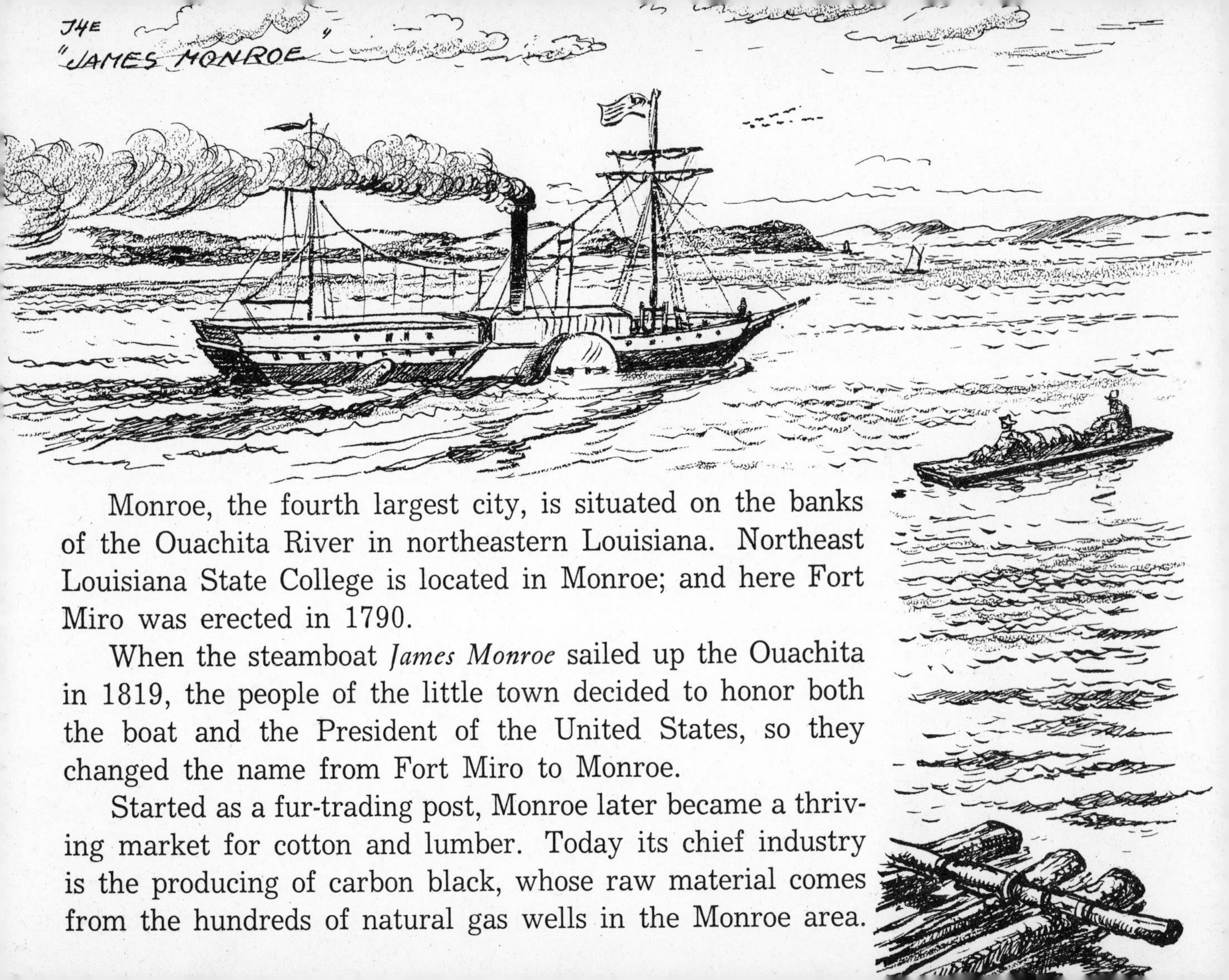

Monroe, the fourth largest city, is situated on the banks of the Ouachita River in northeastern Louisiana. Northeast Louisiana State College is located in Monroe; and here Fort Miro was erected in 1790.

When the steamboat *James Monroe* sailed up the Ouachita in 1819, the people of the little town decided to honor both the boat and the President of the United States, so they changed the name from Fort Miro to Monroe.

Started as a fur-trading post, Monroe later became a thriving market for cotton and lumber. Today its chief industry is the producing of carbon black, whose raw material comes from the hundreds of natural gas wells in the Monroe area.

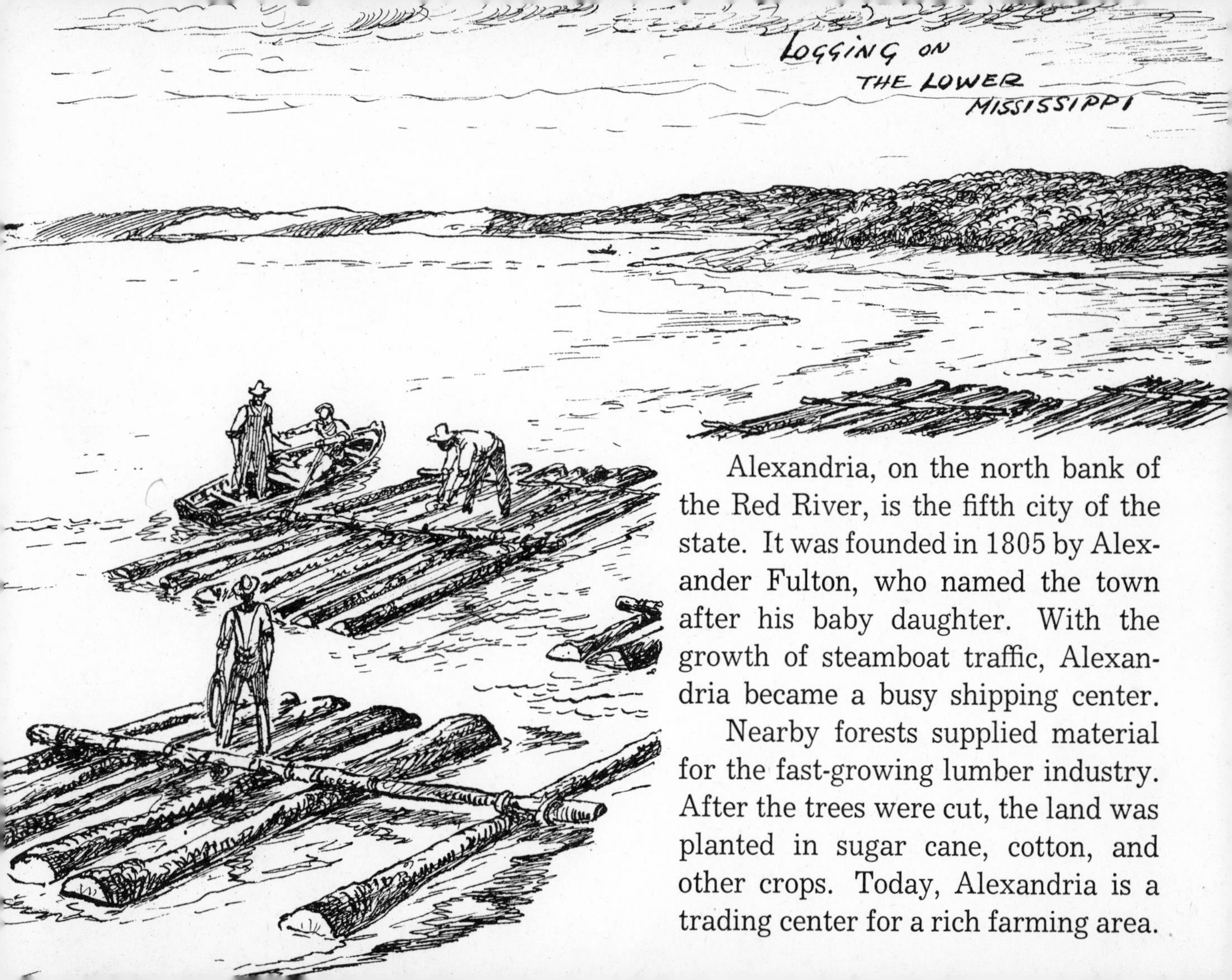

Alexandria, on the north bank of the Red River, is the fifth city of the state. It was founded in 1805 by Alexander Fulton, who named the town after his baby daughter. With the growth of steamboat traffic, Alexandria became a busy shipping center.

Nearby forests supplied material for the fast-growing lumber industry. After the trees were cut, the land was planted in sugar cane, cotton, and other crops. Today, Alexandria is a trading center for a rich farming area.

Across the Red River is the residential city of Pineville, which is closely linked to Alexandria in social and civic activities.

Lake Charles, the sixth city, is in the southwestern corner of the state, only thirty-seven miles from the Gulf of Mexico.

The city almost surrounds the oval lake, which is two miles wide and three miles long. It combines the western ways of Texas and the old-time French customs brought by its earliest settlers. McNeese State Junior College is located in this city.

Petroleum products, lumber, and rice are shipped from its deep-water port. Chemicals, turpentine, and synthetic rubber are important industries here. A large meat-packing plant buys millions of dollars worth of the cattle raised in the state.

Lafayette, in south-central Louisiana, is the center for a rich mineral and farming area. Corn and rice, sugar cane, cotton, and sweet potatoes are grown in abundance. Nearby, salt and sulphur are mined, and there are many oil wells.

Many families in Lafayette still speak French and follow the old French customs. Southwestern Louisiana Institute, established in 1901, now has about three thousand students.

Natchitoches (pronounced Nak-a-tosh) was established as a French trading and military post in 1714. It is thus the oldest town in the state, and still retains many of the romantic traditions of the past. It was named for an Indian tribe of the Caddo family.

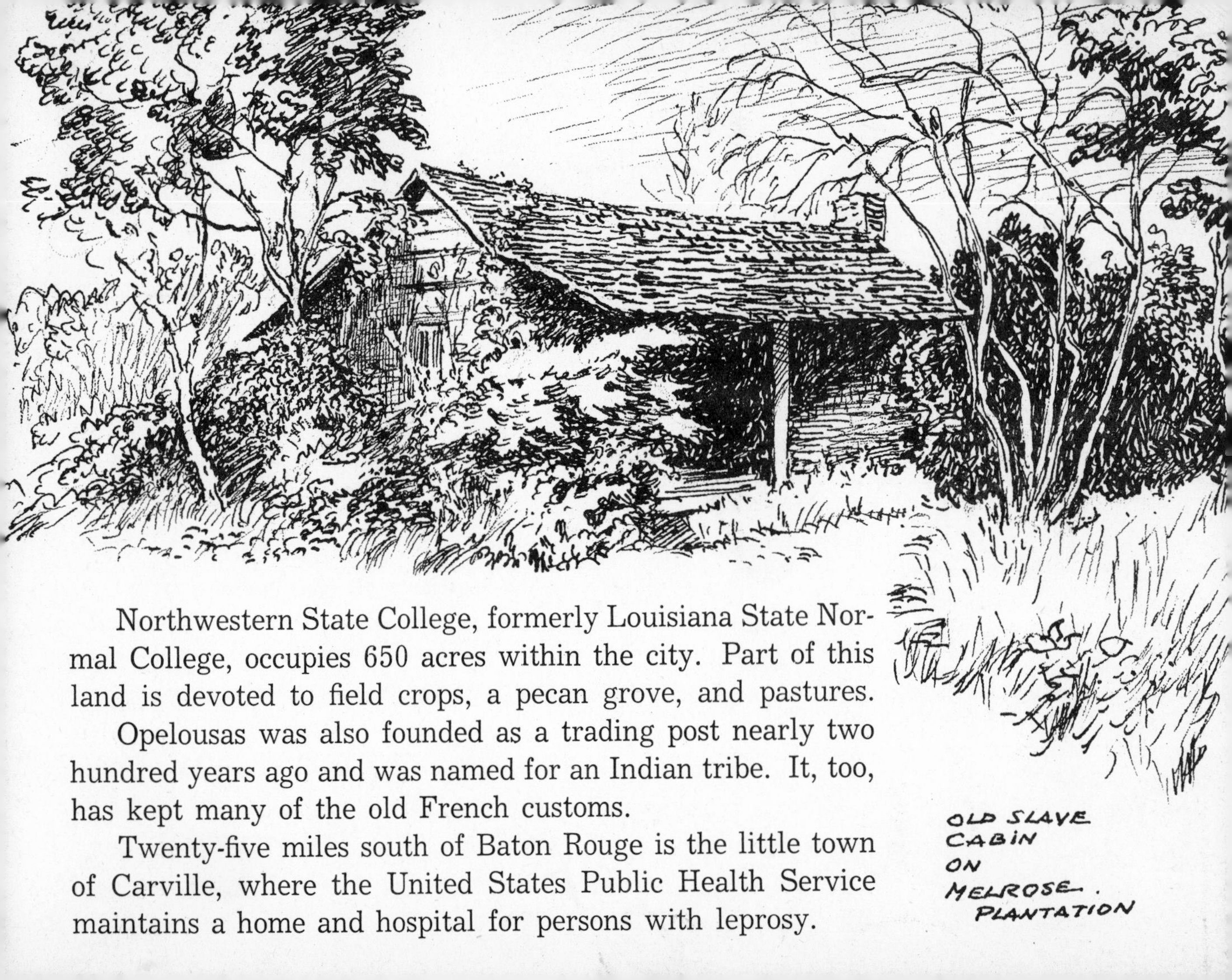

Northwestern State College, formerly Louisiana State Normal College, occupies 650 acres within the city. Part of this land is devoted to field crops, a pecan grove, and pastures.

Opelousas was also founded as a trading post nearly two hundred years ago and was named for an Indian tribe. It, too, has kept many of the old French customs.

Twenty-five miles south of Baton Rouge is the little town of Carville, where the United States Public Health Service maintains a home and hospital for persons with leprosy.

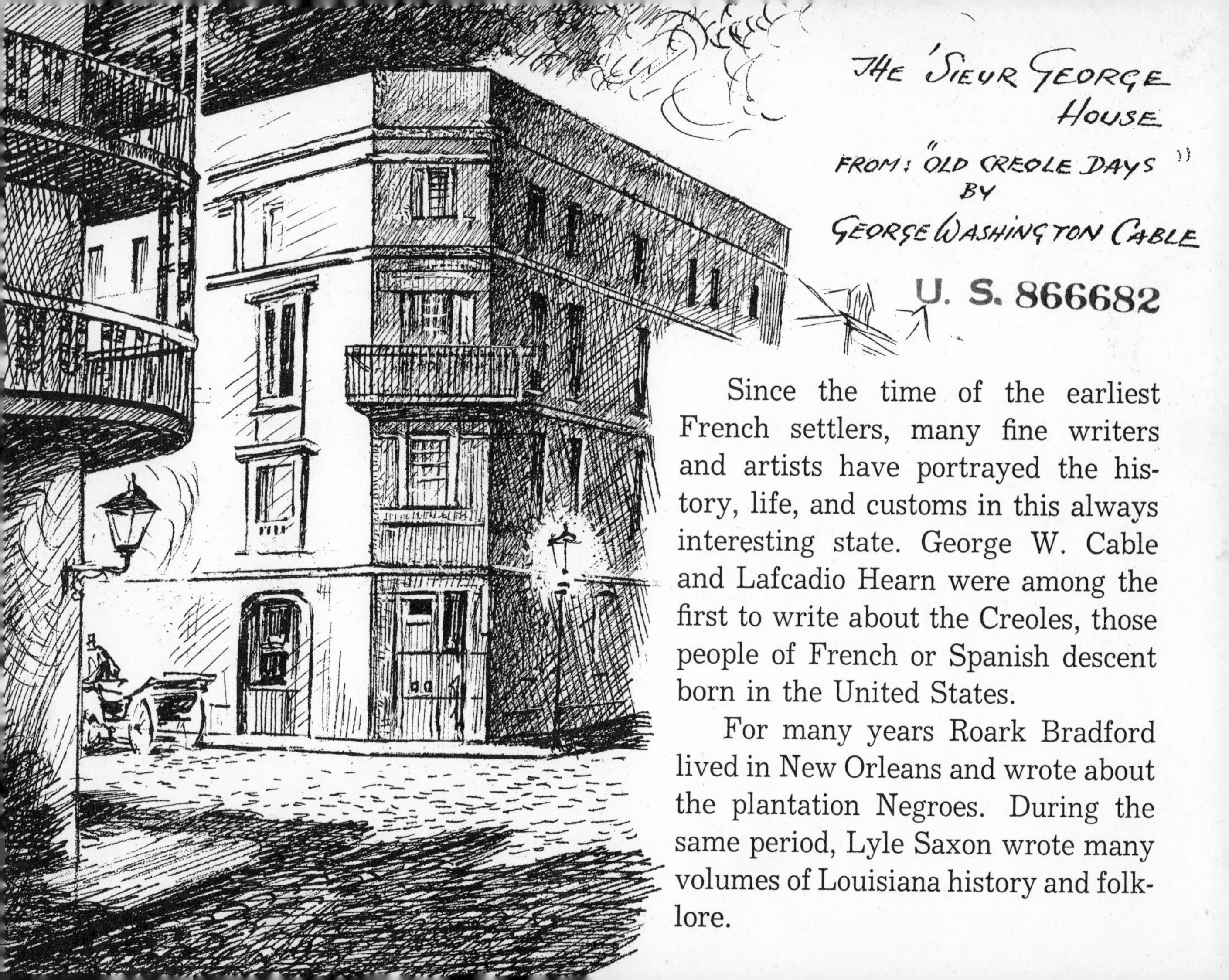

Since the time of the earliest French settlers, many fine writers and artists have portrayed the history, life, and customs in this always interesting state. George W. Cable and Lafcadio Hearn were among the first to write about the Creoles, those people of French or Spanish descent born in the United States.

For many years Roark Bradford lived in New Orleans and wrote about the plantation Negroes. During the same period, Lyle Saxon wrote many volumes of Louisiana history and folklore.

Today, Louisiana forms the background for many of the novels by Frances Parkinson Keyes, Gwen Bristow, and Harnett Kane, all of whom live in the state.

New Orleans has long been the home of jazz music. It is also the home of classical music and has two symphony orchestras. The New Orleans Opera Association continues the tradition of the old French Opera House and gives six or more grand opera performances each year.

The Louisiana of today is rich, enterprising, and alert to modern needs. Yet its citizens do not forget the fine background of history, tradition, and culture that make Louisiana one of the most interesting states in our nation.